A Christian is not one who has stopped all sinning, but one who has begun to feel a new longing – for the Saviour. A heart that desires Jesus is alive and growing. As Augustine taught us long ago, 'Yearning makes the heart deep.' So our theme at the Keswick Convention 2019 is wonderfully profound, and this study guide can help us all go deep.
Ray Ortlund, author and senior pastor, Immanuel Church, Nashville, Tennessee

God has made us for more than just this world, but sometimes our desires can feel overwhelming or even wrong – and, indeed, they may be wrong. In this Keswick study guide, Elizabeth considers some of our God-given longings and shows how only he can satisfy them. Suited for individual or group settings, the studies are rich in biblical truth as well as practical application (with helpful leaders' notes and further reading). They're short but powerful, and will minister to both your head and heart.
Emma Scrivener, author, speaker and blogger

Our hearts so easily go astray. We desire things that aren't good for us – we 'over-desire' things that are – and, in the process, we all too often lose sight of the God who deserves our all. In these six clear and accessible studies, we are called to re-orientate and begin to enjoy God again in all his glory. Whether we're studying alone, with a friend or in a group, there is a wealth of Scripture here to help us long for our Saviour – and keep on longing – until that day we are perfectly fulfilled in him.
Helen Thorne, Director of Training and Mentoring, London City Mission, author and trustee, Biblical Counselling UK

D1584674

Longing

Elizabeth McQuoid

BIBLE STUDY RESOURCES FOR
INDIVIDUALS OR SMALL GROUPS

INTER-VARSITY PRESS
36 Causton Street, London SW1P 4ST, England
Email: ivp@ivpbooks.com
Website: www.ivpbooks.com

First published 2019

British Library Cataloguing-in-Publication Data
A catalogue record for this book is available from the British Library.

ISBN: 978–1–78359–934–9
eBook ISBN: 978–1–78359–935–6

Set in Warnock

Typeset in Great Britain by CRB Associates, Potterhanworth, Lincolnshire
Printed in Great Britain by Ashford Colour Press Ltd, Gosport, Hampshire

Inter-Varsity Press publishes Christian books that are true to the Bible and that communicate the gospel, develop discipleship and strengthen the church for its mission in the world.

IVP originated within the Inter-Varsity Fellowship, now the Universities and Colleges Christian Fellowship, a student movement connecting Christian Unions in universities and colleges throughout Great Britain, and a member movement of the International Fellowship of Evangelical Students. Website: www.uccf.org.uk. That historic association is maintained, and all senior IVP staff and committee members subscribe to the UCCF Basis of Faith.

Contents

Introduction

As I write this, I am longing for some help for my son with special needs. I've pursued every avenue, sat in endless meetings stating his case, but practical help remains as elusive as ever. And I'm longing for my boys to love and serve God wholeheartedly. I long that my life would make the Lord Jesus attractive to them, that they would see him in me, and not remember the yelling to hurry up and get ready for school, my grumpiness at yet another load of laundry, or my short fuse at the end of a long day. I long to be able to sit down for a catch-up with my sister who lives far away. I long for more hours in the day, a bit more sun in the Scottish sky . . .

Your desires may be different from mine, but each one of us, from the staunchest atheist to the youngest child, longs for something. God made us this way; it's how we are wired. Our desires reflect humanity's longing to be happy, to be whole, to belong, for intimacy, for beauty, to be thrilled and fascinated. We can't stop yearning – indeed, we shouldn't even try.

Contemporary culture and the smiley pictures on Facebook want us to believe that family, friends, a lucrative career and an exotic holiday will satisfy these longings. These may well bring much joy, but the satisfaction is temporary and leaves us longing for more. Even the very best sunset, the very best love, the very best experiences are only 'good images of what we really desire . . . For they are not the thing itself; they are only the scent of a flower we have not found, the echo of a tune we have not heard, news from a country we have never yet visited' (C. S. Lewis, *The Weight of Glory*, p. 31). The best that all this world offers will leave us restless and dissatisfied because we were only ever designed to find our satisfaction in God. We sin and become idol worshippers when we look anywhere else.

But why would we sip saltwater when Jesus himself is the ultimate thirst-quencher? He promises that we can find complete satisfaction in him, that our deepest longings will be fulfilled: 'I am the bread of life. Whoever comes to me will never go hungry, and whoever believes in me will never be thirsty . . . Let anyone who is thirsty come to me and drink' (John 6:35; 7:37).

And when we come to him, 'hungering and thirsting for righteousness' (Matthew 5:6), something amazing happens. Not only do we find true satisfaction and discover that God meets our deepest need, but our capacity, our appetite, our longing for him, grows. The more we feast on God, the more of him we want. And his riches are inexhaustible!

One day our longings will fully and finally be satisfied. In the new heavens and the new earth, and in the presence of God himself, our yearning days will be done.

> For the Lamb at the centre of the throne will be their shepherd;
> 'he will lead them to springs of living water.'
> (Revelation 7:17)

Until then, guard your heart; train your desires to be for God alone. Slake your thirst in him, growing ever more thirsty, as you press on in obedience and look forward to that final glorious day when faith gives way to sight and we see him face to face.

Countless books have been written on the topics addressed in these sessions, and no doubt many more will be written as Christians continue to wrestle with these complex and important issues. This study guide is not intended to be exhaustive. Rather, its aim is to help us think biblically as a foundation for further exploration of the themes.

SESSION 1

Longing for God . . .
to answer my prayers

▶ GETTING STARTED

'If only God would . . .'

What did you pray for this morning? A spouse, a job, good health . . . You may be praying for something that is good and right, like release from addiction or your child's salvation, but even then God does not seem to answer your prayers.

In our sadness and confusion, the Psalms provide good company. They are packed with examples of people crying out for God's intervention, and their complaints give words for our anger, hurt and despair. The Psalms show us God can deal with our raw emotions, but, if you read on, they also challenge our perspective. Sometimes we are so consumed by what we want God to do for us that we lose sight of him, and our desires actually steal our affection for him. Perhaps unanswered prayers are God's way to awaken our longing for something far greater: himself.

READ *Psalm 13*

¹ *How long, LORD? Will you forget me for ever?*
  How long will you hide your face from me?
² *How long must I wrestle with my thoughts*
    and day after day have sorrow in my heart?
    How long will my enemy triumph over me?
³ *Look on me and answer, LORD my God.*
    Give light to my eyes, or I will sleep in death,
⁴ *and my enemy will say, 'I have overcome him,'*
    and my foes will rejoice when I fall.
⁵ *But I trust in your unfailing love;*
    my heart rejoices in your salvation.
⁶ *I will sing the LORD's praise,*
    for he has been good to me.

FOCUS ON THE THEME

1. What are you longing for at the moment? What prayers do you wish God would answer?

WHAT DOES THE BIBLE SAY?

2. According to verses 1–4, what is David, the writer of this psalm, longing for?

3. How would you describe David's state of mind in verses 1–4?

4. In the face of unanswered prayer, how does David respond
    in verses 5–6?

◎ GOING DEEPER

5. What kind of things have other believers asked God for? Look at:
    *   Nehemiah 2:1–5

    *   2 Corinthians 12:7–8

    *   Ephesians 6:19

6. Why may God not always answer our prayers? See 2 Corinthians 12:7–9 and Job 38:1–7; 42:1–6.

7. According to 1 John 3:1–3, why should we not be surprised at unmet desires and unfulfilled longings?

Prayer [is not] merely a way to get things from God, but . . . a way to get more of God himself. Prayer is a striving to 'take hold of God' (Isaiah 64:7) the way in ancient times people took hold of a cloak of a great man as they appealed to him, or the way in modern times we embrace someone to show love.

(Tim Keller, *Prayer*, p. 21)

 LIVING IT OUT

8. How can we make sure our prayers stay focused on God rather than becoming like a shopping list of requests?

9. If it is appropriate, share what God is teaching you through your unanswered prayers.

10. In what practical ways can we mirror David's response in verses 5–6 of Psalm 13?

The problem is if God is not the starting point, then our own perceived emotional needs become the drivers and sole focus of our prayer . . . We should not decide how to pray based on the experiences and feelings we want. Instead, we should do everything possible to behold our God as he is, and prayer will follow. The more clearly we grasp who God is, the more our prayer is shaped and determined accordingly.

(Tim Keller, *Prayer*, pp. 61–62)

▲ PRAYER TIME

In reality there are no unanswered prayers. God hears you every time you pray. He may say 'no' if you are asking with selfish motives, or for something that would do you no good. With hindsight we'll be glad God said 'no', because he sees the bigger picture, the eternal perspective, and he knows what furthers his good purpose. He might say 'wait' because it is not the right time for what you're asking, or because he wants to stretch your faith as you learn to trust him more. Or he might say 'yes'!

Speak to God honestly about the requests you mentioned in question 1. Ask him to answer your prayers according to his will (Luke 22:42). But don't stop there. Pray that you would be satisfied in God, not just in the gifts he gives. Ask him to transform your longings so that your deeper desire is for him alone.

⬤ FURTHER STUDY

If you want to give your prayer life a boost, and explore more about how and what to pray, any of the following books would be helpful:

Tim Chester, *You Can Pray* (IVP, 2014)
Phillip Jensen and Tony Payne, *Prayer and the Voice of God* (Matthias Media, 2006)
Tim Keller, *Prayer: Experiencing Awe and Intimacy with God* (Hodder & Stoughton, 2014)
Mike Reeves, *Enjoy Your Prayer Life* (10Publishing, 2014)

SESSION 2

Longing for God . . . to forgive me

▶ GETTING STARTED

'Oh, why did I mess it up – again?' We kick ourselves. The words may be unspoken, but they are no less real.

Guilt, sadness, shame. All these emotions swirl within us when we realize that once again we've let God down. We lost our temper, gossiped with a friend, gave in to that 'comforting', habitual sin. We know we are saved, but our fellowship with God is disturbed, and we feel estranged from him. Satan whispers in our ear that maybe this time our sin is too big for God to forgive, that other Christians would keep their distance if they knew what we'd done.

Despair may seem close at hand, but forgiveness is within reach. Christ's arms outstretched on the cross invite us to come to him for cleansing. His death paid the penalty for our sins once and for all, past, present and future. But repentance isn't a one-time deal. Daily we need to apply God's forgiveness directly to our sin. The Puritans called it 'renewing our repentance'. If you are longing for cleansing, for forgiveness, for spiritual transformation, there is nowhere else to turn.

READ *Psalm 51:1-13*

¹ Have mercy on me, O God,
     according to your unfailing love;
according to your great compassion
     blot out my transgressions.
² Wash away all my iniquity
     and cleanse me from my sin.
³ For I know my transgressions,
     and my sin is always before me.
⁴ Against you, you only, have I sinned
     and done what is evil in your sight;
so you are right in your verdict
     and justified when you judge.
⁵ Surely I was sinful at birth,
     sinful from the time my mother conceived me.
⁶ Yet you desired faithfulness even in the womb;
     you taught me wisdom in that secret place.
⁷ Cleanse me with hyssop, and I shall be clean;
     wash me, and I shall be whiter than snow.
⁸ Let me hear joy and gladness;
     let the bones you have crushed rejoice.
⁹ Hide your face from my sins
     and blot out all my iniquity.
¹⁰ Create in me a pure heart, O God,
     and renew a steadfast spirit within me.
¹¹ Do not cast me from your presence
     or take your Holy Spirit from me.
¹² Restore to me the joy of your salvation
     and grant me a willing spirit, to sustain me.
¹³ Then I will teach transgressors your ways,
     so that sinners will turn back to you.

 FOCUS ON THE THEME

1. 'If we confess our sins, he is faithful and just and will forgive us our sins and purify us from all unrighteousness' (1 John 1:9). Why, then, do we struggle to believe and accept God's forgiveness?

WHAT DOES THE BIBLE SAY?

2. What does David ask for in verses 1–2?

3. In verses 3–6 how does David acknowledge the seriousness of his sin?

4. How do we know David wants deep transformation, real spiritual renewal? Look at verses 10–13.

◉ GOING DEEPER

5. Scan Psalm 40.

   (a) How does David describe the despair of sin (verses 2, 12, 17)?

   (b) What are the results of forgiveness (verses 3, 6–10)?

6. According to Paul in Romans 3:23–26, how much does forgiveness cost?

7. What does God do when he forgives us? Look at:
   - Isaiah 6:6–7

   - Isaiah 43:25

- Philippians 3:9

8. Does forgiveness mean no consequences? See 2 Samuel 12:13–14.

♥ LIVING IT OUT

9. How should we deal with lingering feelings of guilt?

God [is] eager to put away sins. Because the sacrifice of His Son is of such infinite value, He delights to apply it to sinful men and women. God is not a reluctant forgiver; He is a joyous one. His justice having been satisfied and His wrath having been exhausted, He is now eager to extend His forgiveness to all who trust in His Son as their propitiatory sacrifice. He hurls our sins overboard (Micah 7:19). Corrie ten Boom, a dear saint of the last century, used to say, 'And then he puts up a sign saying, "No fishing allowed."' Why would she say that? Because she knew that we tend to drag up our old sins, that we tend to live under a vague sense of guilt. She knew that we are not nearly as vigorous in appropriating God's forgiveness as He is in extending it. Consequently, instead of living in the sunshine of God's forgiveness through Christ, we tend to live under an overcast sky of guilt most of the time.

(Jerry Bridges, *The Gospel for Real Life,* p. 67)

10. According to the Bible passages you have studied this session, what practical measures can you put in place to avoid falling into familiar patterns of sin? Feel free to suggest any other ideas with your group!

 PRAYER TIME

Lord, high and holy, meek and lowly, Thou hast brought me to the valley of vision, where I live in the depths but see Thee in the heights; hemmed in by mountains of sin I behold Thy glory. Let me learn by paradox that the way down is the way up, that to be low is to be high, that the broken heart is the healed heart, that the contrite spirit is the rejoicing spirit, that the repenting soul is the victorious soul, that to have nothing is to possess all, that to bear the cross is to wear the crown, that to give is to receive, that the valley is the place of vision. Lord, in the daytime stars can be seen from deepest wells, and the deeper the wells, the brighter Thy stars shine; let me find Thy light in my darkness, Thy life in my death, Thy joy in my sorrow, Thy grace in my sin, Thy riches in my poverty, Thy glory in my valley.

(Arthur Bennett [ed.], *The Valley of Vision*, p. XV)

 FURTHER STUDY

Forgiveness – God's forgiveness of us and our forgiveness of others – is a huge topic. If you would like to explore it further, you may find the following books helpful:

Chris Braun, *Unpacking Forgiveness: Biblical Answers for Complex Questions and Deep Wounds* (Crossway, 2008)
Michael Jensen, *Is Forgiveness Really Free?* (The Good Book Company, 2014)

Julia Marsden, *Forgiveness* (10Publishing, 2014)

John Stott, *Confess Your Sins: The Way of Reconciliation* (Eerdmans, 2017)

Will van der Hart and Rob Waller, *The Guilt Book: A Path to Grace and Freedom* (IVP, 2014)

Longing for God . . . when my heart has grown cold

▶ GETTING STARTED

'If only I could feel the way I did when I became a Christian / led that summer mission / celebrated Easter over a meal with my home group.'

In 1964 the Righteous Brothers recorded a song called 'You've Lost that Lovin' Feelin'. As believers, sometimes we too lose the 'feelin'. Feelings can be fleeting, or can depend upon our health and circumstances. But sometimes it's more than that. Maybe your Bible reading was getting dry, so you neglected it. God didn't seem to be answering your prayers, so you stopped praying. In church you feel overused and underappreciated. Busyness has sucked the joy out of your worship, and your Christian life, which once was technicolour, has faded to black and white. No-one else may have noticed – you're still serving in church and involved in various rotas and ministries – but *you* know that your relationship with God is not what it once was. Your devotion feels skin-deep. You've stopped longing for God.

Is there a way back? Is it possible to recover the love you once had?

READ Revelation 2:1-7

¹ 'To the angel of the church in Ephesus write:

These are the words of him who holds the seven stars in his right hand and walks among the seven golden lampstands. ² I know your deeds, your hard work and your perseverance. I know that you cannot tolerate wicked people, that you have tested those who claim to be apostles but are not, and have found them false. ³ You have persevered and have endured hardships for my name, and have not grown weary.

⁴ Yet I hold this against you: you have forsaken the love you had at first. ⁵ Consider how far you have fallen! Repent and do the things you did at first. If you do not repent, I will come to you and remove your lampstand from its place. ⁶ But you have this in your favour: you hate the practices of the Nicolaitans, which I also hate.

⁷ Whoever has ears, let them hear what the Spirit says to the churches. To the one who is victorious, I will give the right to eat from the tree of life, which is in the paradise of God.

 FOCUS ON THE THEME

1. Think back over the times when you have drifted away from God. What have been the triggers?

If life is a river, then pursuing Christ requires swimming upstream. When we stop swimming, or actively following Him, we automatically begin to be swept downstream.

(Francis Chan, *Crazy Love*, p. 94)

![Q] WHAT DOES THE BIBLE SAY?

2. According to verses 2–3, what were the Ephesian Christians
    doing right?

3. What was their one failure?

4. Look at verse 5. What did God command them to do to renew their
    love? Consider what this might look like in practice.

*People do not drift toward holiness. Apart from grace-driven effort, people
do not gravitate toward godliness, prayer, obedience to Scripture, faith, and
delight in the Lord. We drift toward compromise and call it tolerance; we
drift toward disobedience and call it freedom; we drift toward superstition
and call it faith. We cherish the indiscipline of lost self-control and call
it relaxation; we slouch toward prayerlessness and delude ourselves into
thinking we have escaped legalism; we slide toward godlessness and
convince ourselves we have been liberated.*

(Don Carson, *For the Love of God*, Volume 2, January 23)

◎ GOING DEEPER

5. The letter to the Hebrews describes the Israelites' rebellion after God had rescued them from Egypt. Chapter 3:10 could describe us too: 'Their hearts are always going astray.' How can we make sure we don't imitate the Israelites' disobedience, and instead recover our love for God? Look at:

    • Hebrews 2:1

    • Hebrews 3:7–8

    • Hebrews 3:12–13

6. Scan Luke 24:13–35. How can our hearts 'burn within us', like the two disciples on the road to Emmaus?

7. If we long to recover our heart affection for God, what does he promise us?
    - James 4:8

    - Micah 7:18–19

    - Lamentations 3:22–23

♥ LIVING IT OUT

8. 'Where your treasure is, there your heart will be also' (Matthew 6:21). Be honest: what do you treasure? Are those treasures drawing you towards, or away from, loving God as you should?

9. 'Repent and do the things you did at first' (Revelation 2:4–5). What did you do when you first loved Jesus? What practices and habits do you need to start cultivating again?

10. As believers, we are supposed to spur one another on to love God more, but often we are content to settle for the status quo. We don't object to mediocre discipleship as long as we're surrounded by like-minded friends! How can you break this mindset? How can you create an environment in your small group or church where together you strive for holiness more and more?

For all the ill that Satan can do, when God describes what keeps us from the banquet table of his love, it is a piece of land, a yoke of oxen and a wife (Luke 14:18–20). The greatest adversary of love to God is not his enemies but his gifts. And the most deadly appetites are not for the poison of evil, but for the simple pleasures of earth . . . These are not vices. They are gifts of God. They are your basic meat and potatoes and coffee and gardening, and reading and decorating and travelling and investing and TV watching and Internet-surfing and shopping and exercising and collecting and talking. And all of them can be deadly substitutes for God.

(John Piper, *A Hunger for God*, pp. 14–15)

 PRAYER TIME

Restore us to yourself, LORD, that we may return;
renew our days as of old.
(Lamentations 5:21)

 FURTHER STUDY

The stark reality is that when God isn't chief in our affections, we have given our heart to an idol. Our idols may not look like those of the Israelites, made of wood or metal, but they are nevertheless very real and equally as dangerous. The following books will not be easy reading, but they will help you identify and deal with what is stealing your love for God.

Elyse Fitzpatrick, *Idols of the Heart: Learning to Long for God Alone* (P&R Publishing, 2016)

Julian Hardyman, *Idols: God's Battle for Our Hearts* (IVP, 2011)

Steve Hoppe, *Sipping Saltwater: How to Find Satisfaction in a World of Thirst* (The Good Book Company, 2017)

Paul Mallard, *Staying Fresh: Serving with Joy* (IVP, 2015)

SESSION 4

Longing for God . . . to take me deeper

▶ GETTING STARTED

Does God feel distant? If there is a sin you're harbouring, or you've stopped reading your Bible and praying, then it's hardly surprising. But sometimes there is no obvious reason why God feels far away. Imagine teaching a child to ride a bike. At first, you're holding the back of the bike, cheering her on, but, after a while you slowly release your hand and run alongside her. You're still there but you've got to take your hand away so the child learns to ride. Sometimes God appears to take his hand away to teach us to trust him, to stretch our faith, to make us long for him even more.

David was in the desert, fleeing from his rebellious son Absalom. He doesn't appear to have any sin blocking his relationship with God, but the parched land prompted him to realize his thirst for God. Amazingly, in this hostile environment, and with his heart breaking over his family situation, David experienced startling clarity about what he needed most: a deeper experience of God.

READ *Psalm 63*

¹ *You, God, are my God,*
earnestly I seek you;
I thirst for you,
my whole being longs for you,
in a dry and parched land
where there is no water.
² *I have seen you in the sanctuary*
and beheld your power and your glory.
³ *Because your love is better than life,*
my lips will glorify you.
⁴ *I will praise you as long as I live,*
and in your name I will lift up my hands.
⁵ *I will be satisfied as with the richest of foods;*
with singing lips my mouth will praise you.
⁶ *On my bed I remember you;*
I think of you through the watches of the night.
⁷ *Because you are my help,*
I sing in the shadow of your wings.
⁸ *I cling to you;*
your right hand upholds me.
⁹ *Those who want to kill me will be destroyed;*
they will go down to the depths of the earth.
¹⁰ *They will be given over to the sword*
and become food for jackals.
¹¹ *But the king will rejoice in God;*
all who swear by God will glory in him,
while the mouths of liars will be silenced.

FOCUS ON THE THEME

1. Think back to a time when you longed for a deeper, more satisfying experience of God. What circumstances provoked that longing for God?

WHAT DOES THE BIBLE SAY?

2. How does the psalmist describe
    *   His longing for God (verse 1)?

    *   Intimate communion with God (verse 5)?

3. What motivates David's longing? See verse 2.

4. What determined action is David taking to satisfy his desire for God? See verses 3–8, 11.

What makes life worthwhile is having a big enough objective, something which catches our imagination and lays hold of our allegiance, and this the Christian has in a way that no other person has. For what higher, more exalted, and more compelling goal can there be than to know God?

(J. I. Packer, *Knowing God*, p. 36)

◎ GOING DEEPER

5. How do the following images describe the type of relationship God wants with us?

- Jesus as the bridegroom (Isaiah 62:5)

- Jesus as the bread of life (John 6:35)

- Jesus as the vine (John 15:1–4)

- Jesus as the host (Psalm 23:5)

6. Look at Ephesians 3:16–19 and 4:11–13 where Paul talks about the 'fullness of God' and the 'fullness of Christ'. How can we obtain this fullness?

7. Even the apostle Paul, who was such a dedicated follower of Christ, declared, 'I want to know Christ' (Philippians 3:10–11). What would this deeper experience of God entail?

Forgetting what is behind and straining towards what is ahead, I press on towards the goal to win the prize for which God has called me heavenwards in Christ Jesus.

(Philippians 3:13–14)

 **LIVING IT OUT**

8. What holds you back from wanting more of God?

9. What determined action do you need to take in order to pursue more of God?

10. In his letters Paul encourages this pursuit of Christ to be a collective pursuit, a whole-church endeavour. How can you encourage one another in this?

One might think that those who feast most often on communion with God are least hungry. They turn often from the innocent pleasures of the world to linger more directly in the presence of God through the revelation of his Word. And there they eat the Bread of Heaven and drink the Living Water by meditation and faith. But, paradoxically, it is not so that they are the least hungry saints. The opposite is the case. The strongest, most mature Christians I have ever met are the hungriest for God. It might seem that those who eat most would be least hungry. But that's not the way it works with an inexhaustible fountain, and an infinite feast, and a glorious Lord. When you take your stand on the finished work of God in Christ, and begin to drink at the River of Life and eat the Bread of Heaven, and know that you have found the end of all your longings, you only get hungrier for God.

(John Piper, *A Hunger for God*, p. 23)

▲ PRAYER TIME

'You, God, are my God.' Like the psalmist, reaffirm your allegiance to God and his commitment to you. Reflect on all the evidence of God's love towards you, and respond in praise and thanksgiving.

My God, give me yourself, restore yourself to me. See, I love you, and if it is too little, let me love you more strongly ... Make my life run to your embraces, and not to turn away until it lies hidden 'in the secret place of your presence' (Psalm 31:20).
(St Augustine, *The Confessions*, p. 278)

 **FURTHER STUDY**

Give thanks to the LORD for his unfailing love
  and his wonderful deeds for mankind,
for he satisfies the thirsty
  and fills the hungry with good things.
(Psalm 107:8–9)

Look at Psalms 27, 42 and 84. How do they help us learn how to long for God? Consider:

- How the psalmist describes his desire for God
- The truths he declares about God
- The confidence he has in God
- The actions he takes as a result

Pray through these psalms, applying them to your own situation.

SESSION 5

Longing for God . . . to display his glory

▶ GETTING STARTED

What comes to mind when you hear the word 'glory'?

The prophet Ezekiel saw God's glory and fell face down, lost for words.

No wonder we struggle to define 'glory'. It's beyond explanation and comprehension because it is the sum of who God is, all his perfect attributes on display. Creation declares God's glory, the angels at Jesus' birth sang about it, the Israelites followed it, the temple and tabernacle were filled with it, Jesus revealed it, and soon it will light up the new heavens and new earth. Now we catch glimpses of God's glory, but one day his infinite worth will be revealed and he'll receive the worship he's due.

Until then we long to see God's character – his holiness, justice, wisdom and compassion – reflected in our government, courts, big business and media. We long for his glory to be more and more on display in the church and in our lives. Whenever you feel these longings stirring in your heart, remember: this is what you were created for (Isaiah 43:7). God is passionate about his own glory, and he wants you to share his passion.

READ *Isaiah 48:1–11*

¹ 'Listen to this, you descendants of Jacob,
    you who are called by the name of Israel
    and come from the line of Judah,
you who take oaths in the name of the LORD
    and invoke the God of Israel –
    but not in truth or righteousness –
² you who call yourselves citizens of the holy city
    and claim to rely on the God of Israel –
    the LORD Almighty is his name:
³ I foretold the former things long ago,
    my mouth announced them and I made them known;
    then suddenly I acted, and they came to pass.
⁴ For I knew how stubborn you were;
    your neck muscles were iron,
    your forehead was bronze.
⁵ Therefore I told you these things long ago;
    before they happened I announced them to you
so that you could not say,
    'My images brought them about;
    my wooden image and metal god ordained them.'
⁶ You have heard these things; look at them all.
    Will you not admit them?
From now on I will tell you of new things,
    of hidden things unknown to you.
⁷ They are created now, and not long ago;
    you have not heard of them before today.
So you cannot say,
    'Yes, I knew of them.'
⁸ You have neither heard nor understood;
    from of old your ears have not been open.
Well do I know how treacherous you are;
    you were called a rebel from birth.

> ⁹ *For my own name's sake I delay my wrath;*
> *for the sake of my praise I hold it back from you,*
> *so as not to destroy you completely.*
> ¹⁰ *See, I have refined you, though not as silver;*
> *I have tested you in the furnace of affliction.*
> ¹¹ *For my own sake, for my own sake, I do this.*
> *How can I let myself be defamed?*
> *I will not yield my glory to another.*

 # FOCUS ON THE THEME

1. Is it egotistical or acceptable for God to be passionate about his own glory?

 # WHAT DOES THE BIBLE SAY?

2. Describe God's attitude to his own glory, in verse 11.

3. According to verses 1–5, how can people defame God's glory?

4. What is God's response in verses 9–10 to his glory being defamed?

⊙ GOING DEEPER

5. Look at Psalm 96:1–3. What is the mission of God's people?

6. Moses asked to see God's glory, in Exodus 33:18–20. What does God's answer reveal about how his glory is displayed on earth?

7. How can we bring God glory? Look at:
    -   Matthew 5:14–16

    -   John 15:8

- 1 Peter 4:10–11

8. How will God's glory be displayed in the future? What can we look forward to?
    - 1 Peter 5:1

    - John 17:24

    - Habakkuk 2:14

♥ LIVING IT OUT

9. (a) How does your church display God's glory every week?

(b) Consider the needs of your local community. What action could your church or small group take which would meet one of those needs and put God's glory on display?

10. (a) Look back at your answers to question 3. Are there any ways in which you are like the Israelites, belonging to God, but not really living like it?

(b) 'Whatever you do, do it all for the glory of God' (1 Corinthians 10:31). What does that mean in practice? Consider how you could more vividly display God's glory in your:
   • Marriage

   • Family struggles

   • Singleness

- Work

- Finances

- Health issues

- Church life

- Leisure

If you don't feel strong desires for the manifestation of the glory of God, it is not because you have drunk deeply and are satisfied. It is because you have nibbled so long at the table of the world. Your soul is stuffed with small things, and there is no room for the great.

(John Piper, *A Hunger for God*, p. 23)

 **PRAYER TIME**

The prayer Jesus taught his disciples is a prayer for God's glory to be displayed in the world and through our lives. Make this prayer your own.

> *Our Father in heaven,*
> *hallowed be your name,*
> *your kingdom come,*
> *your will be done,*
> *on earth as in heaven.*
> *Give us today our daily bread.*
> *Forgive us our sins*
> *as we forgive those who sin against us.*
> *Lead us not into temptation*
> *but deliver us from evil.*
> *For the kingdom, the power,*
> *and the glory are yours*
> *now and for ever.*
> *Amen.*
> *(Common Worship)*

⬤ **FURTHER STUDY**

Investigate God's passion for his glory and the extent he wants us to share his chief goal. What do the following verses teach us? Exodus 14:4; Isaiah 43:6–7; John 12:27–28; 17:24; Romans 3:23; 9:22–24; 11:36; Ephesians 1:11–12; Revelation 21:23.

Longing for God . . . in Christ to return

▶ GETTING STARTED

'Yes please, but not now . . .'

As a child, I remember looking forward to Jesus' return. But, as December rolled around, I started to pray that he would wait until after Christmas Day! As an adult, I still wrestle with conflicting emotions – longing for Christ's return but still wanting to cling to what I know and to those I love. As our bodies start to creak, and more and more of our loved ones go to be with Jesus, I imagine our focus on the new heavens and the new earth becomes sharper, and this world's grasp on us weakens. But for all of us there is a restlessness, an acknowledgment that things are not as they should be, that we are not home yet. The writer of Ecclesiastes explained this longing as God setting 'eternity in the human heart' (Ecclesiastes 3:11). Sonny, in the film *The Best Exotic Marigold Hotel*, was spot on: 'Everything will be all right in the end, and if it's not all right, it's not the end.' There is much of life that is definitely not all right. But it will be. One day.

READ *Revelation 21:1–7*

¹ *Then I saw 'a new heaven and a new earth,' for the first heaven and the first earth had passed away, and there was no longer any sea.* ² *I saw the Holy City, the new Jerusalem, coming down out of heaven from God, prepared as a bride beautifully dressed for her husband.* ³ *And I heard a loud voice from the throne saying, 'Look! God's dwelling-place is now among the people, and he will dwell with them. They will be his people, and God himself will be with them and be their God.* ⁴ *"He will wipe every tear from their eyes. There will be no more death" or mourning or crying or pain, for the old order of things has passed away.'*

⁵ *He who was seated on the throne said, 'I am making everything new!' Then he said, 'Write this down, for these words are trustworthy and true.'*

⁶ *He said to me: 'It is done. I am the Alpha and the Omega, the Beginning and the End. To the thirsty I will give water without cost from the spring of the water of life.* ⁷ *Those who are victorious will inherit all this, and I will be their God and they will be my children.'*

FOCUS ON THE THEME

1. What are you most looking forward to / anxious about in the new heavens and the new earth?

WHAT DOES THE BIBLE SAY?

2. According to Revelation 21:1–7, how different will the new heaven and earth be from life as it is now?

3. In what ways does John's vision impact on how we live today?

*If I find in myself a desire which no experience in this world can satisfy,
the most probable explanation is that I was made for another world.*

(C. S. Lewis, *Mere Christianity*, p. 35)

⊙ GOING DEEPER

4. Look at 2 Corinthians 5:1–9. Why does Paul say he is longing for his
    heavenly, glorified body?

5. How can he be so sure that this bodily transformation will take
    place (verse 5)?

6. We are urged in 1 John 2:28, 'Dear children, continue in him, so that
    when he appears we may be confident and unashamed before him at
    his coming.' According to 1 John 2:1–29, how do we 'continue' in
    Christ so we are not ashamed when he returns?

7. What does Paul say we should do while we wait for Christ's return? See Titus 2:11–14.

♥ LIVING IT OUT

8. With God's help, what practical action will you take this week to get ready for Christ's return? For example:
   - Repenting of sins you have grown used to

   - Avoiding certain TV programmes and internet sites

   - Asking forgiveness from someone you have hurt

   - Sharing the gospel with a friend, work colleague, child or parent

- Setting up direct debits to support God's work

- Committing to spend time daily in prayer and Bible study

Is not some of the pain and sorrow in this life used in God's providential hand to make us homesick for heaven, to detach us from this world, to prepare us for heaven, to draw our attention to himself, and away from the world of merely physical things?

(Don Carson, in Nancy Guthrie [ed.], *Be Still, My Soul*, p. 116)

9. What is God using in your life to make you 'homesick for heaven'?

10. How can we increase our longing for Christ's return and the establishment of the new heaven and new earth?

The more deeply you walk with Christ, the hungrier you get for Christ . . . the more homesick you get for heaven . . . the more you want 'all the fullness of God' . . . the more you want to be done with sin . . . the more you want the Bridegroom to come again . . . the more you want the Church revived and purified with the beauty of Jesus . . . the more you want a great awakening

to God's reality in the cities . . . the more you want to see the light of the
gospel of the glory of Christ penetrate the darkness of all the unreached
peoples of the world . . . the more you want to see false worldviews yield
to the force of Truth . . . the more you want to see pain relieved and tears
wiped away and death destroyed . . . the more you long for every wrong
to be made right and the justice and grace of God to fill the earth like the
waters cover the sea.

(John Piper, *A Hunger for God*, p. 23)

 PRAYER TIME

In your group, share the names of those individuals you are praying for to
become Christians. Pray together for opportunities to demonstrate God's
love, share the gospel and lead your friends/family to Christ. Ask God to
increase your longing for Christ's return and, with that, a passion for the
salvation of those who don't yet know him.

 FURTHER STUDY

If you would like to learn more about Jesus' second coming and the
eternal home he is preparing for you, study what the Bible says. A good
place to start would be Matthew 24, 1 Thessalonians 4:13 – 5:11 and
2 Peter 3:1–18. Another helpful resource is Randy Alcorn's book, *Heaven*
(Tyndale House, 2007).

Notes for leaders

SESSION 1

SESSION 1

To answer my prayers

1. If this is the first time your group has met, they may be hesitant to share their longings, so be ready to contribute a few ideas. The aim is to raise the issue and acknowledge that we desire many things – some frivolous, others heartfelt – but many of our prayers, even those in line with biblical priorities, will remain apparently unanswered.

2. David is longing to feel: God's presence (verse 1); respite from his personal sorrow and despair (verse 2); renewed strength – in the Old Testament failing eyes often equates to failing strength (verse 3); rescue from his enemy (verse 4).

3. 'How long' is repeated four times in two verses! David is desperate for God to answer his prayers. He is agonizing over God's apparent distance, struggling with his own thoughts, oppressed by the enemy, and consumed by internal and external troubles. He seems lonely and depressed. And yet he recognizes that relief can come only from God. He still acknowledges his personal need of God and calls to the 'LORD my God'.

4. David's prayer remains unanswered, but he draws comfort, peace and joy from God's character. He reflects on God's unfailing love, sings praises to God for all his goodness in the past and present, and therefore he is confident that God has heard his prayer and will provide salvation. In this psalm David's inner turmoil is transformed as he shares his problem with God and gets a renewed perspective on God and his good purposes.

5. These are just a couple of prayer requests we find in the Bible. Nehemiah wanted permission from the king to return to Jerusalem to rebuild the city walls (Nehemiah 2:1–5). Paul was praying for his 'thorn in the flesh' – we don't know exactly what, but some kind of affliction – to be removed from his life (2 Corinthians 12:7). Paul also

asked the Ephesian believers to pray for boldness to proclaim the gospel (Ephesians 6:19).

6. God doesn't always give us what we ask for – to stop us being proud, to keep us trusting in his grace, and because our weakness allows God's power and glory to be on display (2 Corinthians 12:7–9). In Job's case, God did not provide relief from his suffering, or even give any explanation for it. God wanted Job to recognize his incomparable power and sovereignty, and to acknowledge that his ways and purposes are so much higher than ours. At the end of his questioning, Job realized that we do best to trust God with what we don't understand.

7. We are reminded in 1 John 3:1–3 that we are children of God, but we are not home yet. We can't expect all our longings to be fulfilled, because we are still living in a fallen world. We will face rejection, even persecution, just as Jesus did (verse 1). Our bodies are not yet heavenly bodies, so we age and deteriorate (verse 2). We still sin (verse 3).

8. Share practical suggestions together. For example, pray using the acronym ACTS (adoration, confession, thanksgiving, supplication), so that your requests come after you have settled your heart and mind on who God is, and you ask with an attitude of gratefulness for all that he has already done. Perhaps use Paul's prayers in Philippians 1:9–11, Ephesians 1:15–23 and Colossians 1:9–14, in order to keep your focus on God's priorities for you.

9. Bear in mind that we won't always know why God is not answering our prayers, or the specific lessons he wants us to learn. However, we can be sure that he wants to use this not knowing, and everything else that is going on in our lives, to make us more like Jesus (Romans 8:28–29).

10. Many times we want to cry out in anguish like David in verses 1–4. But when we have exhausted our lament, with our hearts breaking, we cling to the character of God. Instead of questioning his love for us, and imagining ourselves abandoned by God (Romans 8:37–39),

we trust his love, acknowledging that he has heard our prayers, and will answer them according to his will, for our good and his glory.

It means we choose to worship God, we keep recounting his goodness to ourselves and others, and we put our confidence in him rather than trying to control or manipulate the situation.

SESSION 2

To forgive me

1. Perhaps we struggle to accept God's forgiveness because: we feel our sin is too big; we feel we must hold on to guilt as a way of punishing ourselves; we don't believe our wrongdoing is so bad that it warrants God's forgiveness; we'd rather earn forgiveness than accept it as a free gift from God; we don't really want to turn our back on sin and change our ways.

2. If necessary, provide the group with some background to Psalm 51. It may be helpful to summarize the events of 2 Samuel 11 – 12. David is putting his hope in the mercy, love and compassion of God, and asking to be cleansed from his sins. He talks about his sins being blotted out, washed away, that is, completely removed. Verse 7 talks again about cleansing. Hyssop was a branch used in the Old Testament by priests to sprinkle blood in cleansing ceremonies. David is asking God to act as a priest and cleanse him from sin.

3. David acknowledges that his sin is always at the forefront of his mind; he can't escape the guilt (verse 3). It was an attack against God. Bathsheba and her husband Uriah were hurt, but the offence was primarily against God (verse 4). David accepts God's verdict on his sin. He doesn't try to justify or excuse himself; he knows God's verdict is justified (verse 4). He acknowledges that his adultery and murder were symptoms of something far worse – his sinful nature (verse 5). He knew God desired faithfulness, and yet he did the exact opposite (verse 6).

He asks God for a 'pure heart' – he wants inner transformation, not just outward respectability. He longs for purity and a spirit of faithfulness, so he won't drift into sin again (verse 10). He pleads for the Holy Spirit to stay with him. Remember, because of King Saul's failures, God removed the Holy Spirit from him in 1 Samuel 16:14, and David was anointed king in his place (verse 11). He asks for joy so that he can then testify to others about God's forgiveness and restoration – his experience of God's grace and mercy was so profound that he couldn't wait to share it with others (verses 12–13).

4. (a) David feels so overwhelmed by sin that he describes it as being in a slimy pit, bogged down in the mud (verse 2). He feels so burdened and boxed in by countless sins that he describes it in physical terms – not being able to see, his heart failing (verse 12). He describes himself as poor and needy – completely at God's mercy for rescue (verse 17).

   (b) He praises God for this latest rescue mission, with a new song. His testimony leads others to know God personally (verse 3). God has opened his ears to hear and be attentive to his Word (verse 6). This could refer to the practice of piercing a servant's ear to the doorpost if he wanted to pledge lifelong obedience to his master (see Exodus 21:6). He is now longing to obey God's will (verse 8). He can't stop praising God and telling people of all God's loving, righteous acts in saving his people (verses 9–10).

5. Romans 3:23–26 says forgiveness is free for us. There is nothing we can do to earn our salvation or contribute to it. It is a free gift of God's grace to us – we simply accept it by faith. However, our salvation cost Jesus the ultimate price. He died in our place, his blood paying the penalty for sin we should have paid.

6. Isaiah 6:6–7: God takes away our sin *and* our guilt. It doesn't just deal with the sinful act, but also the feelings that go along with it. Isaiah 43:25: he not only forgives our sins, but he chooses not to remember them. He is not waiting to dredge up our failures at every opportunity, nor does he hold our sins against us. Philippians 3:9: taking away our sin is only part of the transaction. Forgiveness means God takes my sin, but he also gives me Christ's righteousness. When he looks at me, he does not see my sin, although I am a sinner, but, because of Jesus' death on the cross, he sees me covered in Christ's righteousness.

7. Having realized the gravity of his sin and having repented, David was forgiven by God. He was spared the death penalty his sin deserved.

However, there were disciplinary consequences – his son would die. As believers, having been justified by God, our eternal life is secure. We do not receive the death penalty our sins deserve, because Jesus died in our place. However, we will still face the consequences, the temporal effects, of our sin. This shows how seriously God takes sin, and also his desire for our growth in godliness (Hebrews 12:10–11).

8. Satan likes to remind us of past sin and how easily we fall into temptation. His whispers fuel our guilt, robbing us of joy in our service and salvation. We need to remind ourselves and the devil of passages like Isaiah 6:6–7 and 43:25. We need to come back to the cross and trust Jesus' complete payment for our sins. Ask God to help you believe the gospel and live in the benefit of it. Sing hymns like the one below to remind yourself of your true status:

> *When Satan tempts me to despair*
> *And tells me of the guilt within,*
> *Upward I look and see Him there*
> *Who made an end of all my sin.*
> *Because the sinless Savior died*
> *My sinful soul is counted free.*
> *For God the just is satisfied*
> *To look on Him and pardon me.*
> (Charitie L. Bancroft, 'Before the Throne of God Above', 1863)

9. Reflect frequently on the cost of your salvation (Romans 3:23–26); ask for the Holy Spirit's help (Psalm 51:11); worship in song (Psalm 40:3); spend time daily in repentance (1 John 1:9); avoid tempting situations and people (2 Timothy 2:22); positively pursue holiness by studying and obeying God's Word (Psalms 40:8; 119:9–11); be disciplined about your thoughts (Philippians 4:8); ask for God's wisdom (James 1:5). Avoiding sin involves a two-pronged approach – the things we must not do and the things we must do. Or, as Colossians 3:1–14 explains, using the analogy of clothes, there are dirty clothes we must take off and clean clothes we must put on.

When my heart has grown cold

1. There are any number of things that can negatively impact our love for God: busyness, becoming consumed with career and finances, feeling disappointed in God for some reason, having prolonged periods where Bible reading feels stale, being hurt by other believers, getting involved in some habitual sin, being distracted by a new boyfriend/girlfriend . . . It is worth pointing out that our drift away from God is not usually premeditated and happens gradually. It is not always caused by us doing evil, but simply by allowing good things to take God's place.

2. These believers were saying and doing all the right things. They were working hard for God, persevering under persecution, holding fast to orthodox teaching and weeding out false apostles.

3. Their one failure was that they'd lost their passionate love. It is not clear whether this refers to the love they had for God when they first became believers or their love for one another. It could refer to both. The Ephesian Christians illustrate that it is possible to act like a disciple, being fully involved in church and ministry, without your heart being engaged and devoted to God and his people.

4. The Ephesians were told to do three things which model how our love for God can be restored. First, 'Consider how far you have fallen' – they were to spend time reflecting on the extent and seriousness of their sin, how changed their discipleship was, how estranged from God and other believers they had become. Second, 'Repent' – they were to ask for God's forgiveness and his help to change course and return to obedience. Third, 'do the things you did at first' – they were to go back and do what they had done when they were first converted. Remember the enthusiasm you had when you first became a Christian, that first flush of love for God? Well, do what you did then.

This will certainly involve prayer; Bible reading, study and meditation; daily repentance; meeting with other believers for teaching and Communion; serving; giving to God generously and sharing with others.

5. Hebrews 2:1: we must pay 'careful attention . . . to what we have heard'. From the context, we learn that the author is demanding they pay careful attention to the gospel – 'how shall we escape if we ignore so great a salvation?' (verse 3). We need constantly to retell the gospel to ourselves, and live as if we believe it, if we are to grow in our love for God. Hebrews 3:7–8: we are to listen for the Holy Spirit's prompting and yield to him in obedience to keep our hearts 'soft' towards God. Hebrews 3:12–13: believers are supposed to encourage one another to keep their hearts focused on God and not let sin deceive them into substituting something else for their love of him.

6. Jesus walked along the road with these two disciples, giving them a Bible study. His main point was that the Scriptures were all about him (Luke 24:27). What captivated their affections was an interpretation of Scripture that put Jesus and his finished work at the forefront. Our love for God will not grow cold when we reflect the truths of Scripture in our lives and give Jesus the pre-eminence he deserves.

7. If we long to recover the love we once had for the Lord and restore our relationship with him, he is more than willing to forgive and renew us. James 4:8 promises that God will draw near to us if we draw near to him. Micah 7:18–19 promises that God will forgive us again and show mercy and compassion. From the New Testament, we know it was Christ's death on the cross that dealt completely with our sin. Micah describes this using picture language: God crushing our sin and hurling it into the deepest ocean. Lamentations 3:22–23 promises that God's love, compassion and faithfulness are renewed to us each day. Each day there is a fresh supply of God's riches to provide help and strength to live for him.

8. What we spend time thinking about, doing, investing ourselves in – that is our treasure. Such treasures determine whether our hearts are

turned towards, or away from, God. Even if these treasures are good and right, like family or Christian ministry, if God himself is not our ultimate treasure, then we are idolaters. In short, giving anything other than God first place in our life is idolatry.

9. Think about all the things you did when you were first converted and full of enthusiasm for your new-found faith. Perhaps you journalled, fasted, spent extended time praying and meditating on God's Word, read Christian biographies, kept prayer lists and recorded answered prayer, or you were committed to your church and small group, eager to serve in ministry, passionate about evangelism. Even if you didn't do these things, consider what habits you should cultivate now to restore your love for the Lord.

10. From the Bible verses we have looked at in this study, we know that holiness and love for the Lord are a matter of the heart. It is about us giving God pre-eminence in our daily lives, a relentless personal decision as, with his help, we say 'no' to sin and 'yes' to righteousness (Titus 2:11–14). However, as Hebrews 3:12–13 indicates, there is a role for believers to encourage one another not to 'turn away from the living God' (verse 12). Just by getting together in small groups or as a whole church, worshipping, listening to sermons, we remind ourselves of what and why we believe. Perhaps there are other ways your church community could raise the bar on discipleship: reading and discussing a Christian book with a friend, meeting regularly with someone for accountability and prayer, memorizing Scriptures, learning how to study and apply the Bible better. Is there one practical action you could take as a result of this study?

To take me deeper

1. No-one would wish for difficult circumstances, sadness or suffering, but we need to recognize that often God uses these experiences to deepen our faith and sharpen our focus on him. In dark days we often long for God more, as we realize he is all we have and all we need.

2. David is in the dry and arid desert. His physical thirst becomes a picture of his desperate thirst for God (verse 1). His whole body feels this longing for God. He describes deep intimacy with God like being 'satisfied as with the richest of foods' – like a lavish banquet that nourishes the depths of his soul (verse 5).

3. David had longed for God before, and God had revealed his power and glory to him in the tabernacle. It is because of these past experiences that David longs for something more. Although God is 'the same yesterday and today and for ever' (Hebrews 13:8), our relationship with him, like all relationships, is dynamic, so don't expect to live on a constant spiritual high. Instead, allow these past experiences to remind you how worthwhile pursuing intimacy with God is.

4. David's desire for God is more than just an emotional feeling. The psalm outlines his practical, persistent, determined pursuit of God. He can't see any evidence that God is near, or working in his desperate situation, but David trusts God's covenant love. He is confident that God's love is better than everything else life offers. So he praises God in speech and song, he lifts his hands in worship, and he rejoices in God's help and security. Even in the restlessness of sleepless nights, David keeps his thoughts fixed on God. He describes himself as clinging to God, only able to do so because God upholds him. The ASV version translates verse 8 as 'My soul follows hard after you', which aptly conveys the relentlessness of David's pursuit of God.

5. Bridegroom: Jesus wants an exclusive, passionate, intimate relationship with us. A relationship that provides comfort, security and lasting love. Bread: only Jesus can completely satisfy us and provide the nourishment we need. Vine: Jesus is the source of our life, growth and fruitfulness. He wants us to flourish in dependence on him. Host: Jesus welcomes us. We are no longer his enemies, but friends he wants to spend time with and lavishly provide for. In Bible times a meal signified the bonds of friendship, protection and care, and anointing with oil was a way to honour a guest.

6. Note that the 'fullness of Christ' and the 'fullness of God' (and the 'fullness of the Spirit', Ephesians 5:18) are not separate fullnesses, but the same thing. Neither is it some mystical experience to chase after. The 'fullness of God' is the sum total of who God is, all of his glorious attributes. When we are full of God, our wills, our emotions and our whole being are submitted to him. We are completely satisfied by him. This 'fullness' is what we are aiming for – it is spiritual maturity; it is becoming more and more like Christ. This filling is an ongoing process, as God's resources are infinite. In Ephesians 3:16–19 Paul prays for God to help us grasp his limitless love. We'll never be able to plumb the depths of this love (because it's limitless!), but we can grow in awareness of it, and it is as we do so that we grow in spiritual maturity. Ephesians 4:11–13 explains again that the 'fullness of Christ' is spiritual maturity, becoming like Christ. Together, we become mature by acknowledging and obeying the great truths of Scripture (unity in the faith) and growing in our personal relationship with Christ (the knowledge of the Son of God).

7. When we become Christians, we are united to Christ positionally (Romans 6:1–10). This means that the effects of Christ's death and resurrection are credited to our account, applied on our behalf. But Paul doesn't simply want factual knowledge; he wants to know this resurrection power in daily life and to suffer with and for Christ, even to the point of death. Neither is he interested solely in uplifting experiences. Notice this deeper experience of Christ is both resurrection power and suffering – it is not either/or.

8. Recognizing the cost of being a devoted follower of Christ, the suffering and ridicule we may face, the relationships/pursuits we will have to give up, and the effort involved, can make us pause for thought. It is important to count the cost (Luke 14:25–33). But then, like David, we realize that true satisfaction is found only in Christ. With Simon Peter we admit, 'Lord, to whom shall we go? You have the words of eternal life' (John 6:68).

9. For David, longing for a deeper experience of God meant worshipping him in difficult times, trusting God's goodness when he felt far away. It meant a single passion for God, to the neglect of all else. For Paul, it meant leaving behind his sinful past, not resting on past ministry achievements, but pressing on, with the dedication of a runner intent on winning the race. That meant discipline and hard work, patient perseverance, saying no to things that were 'good' in order to achieve what was 'best' (Philippians 3:13–14). It is trusting God, obeying his commands, putting your faith in his promises (John 14:21). What does this look like in your life? More time devoted to prayer; being disciplined about studying God's Word, even when you don't feel like it; committing to regular attendance at church and home group; reading Christian books; teaming up with an accountability partner; avoiding temptations; fasting and . . . ?

10. Meet up with Christian friends to pray, discuss a Christian book together, text/email words of encouragement and specific prayer requests. Discuss practical ideas that would work for your group.

SESSION 5

To display his glory

1. C. S. Lewis voiced our concerns about God being egotistical: 'The miserable view that God should in any sense need, or crave for, our worship, like a vain woman wanting compliments' (*Reflections on the Psalms*, p. 109). However, this view stems from our human perception of God and our selfish and vain pursuit of personal glory. Because God is perfect, he cannot look beyond himself to anyone or anything greater, and therefore he is worthy of honour. It is right that he is jealous of his glory and won't share it with others. But this does not make God cold and manipulative. His glory is self-giving – just think of the glory of God displayed in the cross of Christ which bought our redemption. And, amazingly, seeking and seeing that glory actually brings us joy.

2. God is passionate for his own glory: it motivates all of his actions. He will not let his name be defamed; he will not let anyone take the glory that belongs to him. He will act to vindicate his name.

3. These people were God's people, but didn't live as if they were. Their prayers and devotion were not heartfelt (verse 1); they claimed to trust in God, but didn't do so (verse 2); they were stubborn and unwilling to submit to God's will and ways (verse 4); they worshipped and attributed God's acts to idols instead of being wholeheartedly committed to him (verse 5).

4. God held back his anger and did not completely destroy the people. But he did send affliction to refine their faith and bring them back to obedience.

5. We have a mandate to declare God's glory throughout the world. We are to praise God with singing and tell people in all nations about the gospel and all that God has done for them. This is an Old Testament

anticipation of the world mission of the New Testament people of God (Matthew 28:16–20).

6. Moses asks to see God's glory, and God responds by talking about, and showing him, his attributes. This means that to reflect God's glory, we need to reflect his attributes. Glorifying God is not about reciting special words or phrases. Rather, it is a life that reflects the attributes of God, a lifestyle consumed with putting his glory on display. It means being like Jesus, who is 'the radiance of God's glory' (Hebrews 1:3).

7. Matthew 5:14–16: like a city built on a hill or a lamp set on a lampstand, glorifying God means we let the light of God's attributes shine before others so that they join us in glorifying him. John 15:8: living fruitful Christian lives glorifies God. In the context of John 15, this fruit is the result of a life rooted and grounded in Christ, which submits to the pruning and discipline of God, is obedient to God's commands and overflows in love. 1 Peter 4:10–11: we glorify God as we use our gifts and talents to serve others, not boasting or confident in ourselves, but depending on his strength and relying on his grace. The New City Catechism, question 6, is helpful on this matter: 'How do we glorify God?' 'We glorify God by enjoying him, loving him, trusting him, and by obeying his will, commands, and law.'

8. 1 Peter 5:1: when Jesus returns, we will share in his glory (see also Romans 8:30). John 17:24: we will see Jesus as he is now, crowned in all his glory at the Father's side (see also Hebrews 2:9). Habakkuk 2:14: God's glory will be evident all over the earth, and everyone will be aware of it.

9. (a) Use your answers to questions 5–7 to inform your ideas here. For example, we declare God's glory when we sing his praises on a Sunday morning; when we display his attributes of love and compassion to elderly members of our congregation through friendship and meals; when we visit and show mercy to those in prison; when we strive for purity in our marriages; when we care

for children and share the gospel with them in weekly clubs; when we seek justice in our communities.

(b) Come up with some concrete plans for how you could serve your community, and in so doing be like that city on a hill, the lamp on a lampstand, displaying God's glory (Matthew 5:14–16). Pray that your 'good deeds' would attract people to Jesus. And that coming to know him personally, they too would glorify God.

10. (a) Use your answers to question 3 to guide your discussion. For example, are you claiming to trust God in a particular area when really you are putting your trust in other people/things or seeking to take control yourself? What are your idols: the people or things taking God's first place in your life? Perhaps your idols are family, work, money, leisure . . . Thank God for showing you your divided heart, and turn back to him in repentance.

(b) Think how you can practically and specifically display God's attributes in these areas of your life. For example, being more patient and less critical with your spouse; intentionally submitting to God's will in suffering and not becoming bitter and irritable; enjoying leisure time as a gift from God and not an excuse to indulge in self-absorbed laziness. Perhaps choose just one area that, with God's help, you will work on this coming week.

SESSION 6

In Christ to return

1. This opening question is intended to allow people to voice their excitement, as well as their anxieties, about the future. Most of us will look forward to no more tears, suffering, disease or wickedness. But some people may worry about being bored in heaven – what will they do? They may worry that their joy of heaven will be tarnished if family or friends are not there. You don't need to answer everyone's concerns now. Hopefully, these issues will be addressed as the study unfolds.

   The main difference will be God's presence with us physically. God will be the sole focus of our attention. There will be no more wickedness (the Old Testament associated the sea with evil), tears, death, mourning, pain or crying. The removal of these things doesn't just indicate that evil is eradicated, but that there will be no memories of the suffering to cause us pain. Our redemption, as well as that of creation, will be fully complete – 'It is done' (Revelation 21:6). Our longing for God will be fully and finally satisfied by God himself.

2. As we grieve, face suffering and, to some extent, deal with opposition to our faith, we remember that God sees and cares about these trials, but they are temporary. This vision of the new heavens and the new earth gives us strength to persevere as we look with hope to the future. With the eyes of faith, we see our salvation is complete. Like those first-century believers, John wants to encourage us that God is 'the Alpha and the Omega' (Revelation 22:13) – he is in control of the beginning and the end of history and everything in between. We can trust him completely. This is the spur we need to press on, to be 'victorious' (Revelation 21:7).

3. Paul is longing for his glorified body because it is made by God, and therefore will be eternal and perfect. This is in contrast to his earthly body which is temporary and subject to frailty and death. He is also

looking forward to his glorified state because it means he will no longer be living by faith, but he will actually be in the presence of God.

4. The indwelling Holy Spirit is a guarantee that the transformation God has started in our lives (2 Corinthians 3:18; Philippians 1:6) will be brought to completion.

5. How do we 'continue' in Christ? Be quick to repent (verse 1); keep his commands (verses 3–5); live as Jesus did (verse 6); love others (verse 10); do God's will, and don't give in to sinful desires, lust after the superficial or be proud of one's achievements (verses 16–17); continue believing the gospel and applying sound teaching to your life (verse 24); 'remain' in Christ, trusting him, being dependent on him, being sustained by him (verse 27); live holy lives, reflecting God's character (verse 29).

6. Because of our future expectation of Christ's return, we have present responsibilities. We must draw on God's grace to live a holy life. This means we turn away from sinful behaviour and thoughts, and we positively pursue godliness. In God's grace, we can mature in self-control, goodness and purity, ready for Christ's return.

7. Encourage the group to make their answers to questions 6 and 7 concrete and personal.

8. Reflect on how present difficulties, grief, the brokenness of our world – all the things which are not 'all right' (to quote Sonny earlier) – help point you to Christ. We can't make light of personal suffering, but consider how suffering can have value, to the extent that it helps us find satisfaction in Christ alone and increases our longing for heaven.

9. Colossians 3:1–3 urges us to set our hearts and minds on 'things above'. The more we consider, meditate, read and pray about Christ's return and the new heavens and new earth, the more this will whet our appetite and shape our priorities. As the John Piper quote indicates, the deeper our relationship with Christ grows, the greater will be our longing for his return and for his glory to be displayed. Come, Lord Jesus!

Books mentioned in the text

Randy Alcorn, *Heaven* (Tyndale House, 2007)

Arthur Bennett (ed.), *The Valley of Vision: A Collection of Puritan Prayers and Devotions* (Banner of Truth, 2002)

Jerry Bridges, *The Gospel for Real Life: Turn to the Liberating Power of the Cross . . . Every Day* (NavPress, 2002)

Don Carson, *For the Love of God, Volume 2* (IVP, 2011)

Francis Chan, *Crazy Love: Overwhelmed by a Relentless God* (David C. Cook, 2013)

Nancy Guthrie (ed.), *Be Still, My Soul* (IVP, 2010)

Collin Hansen (ed.), *The New City Catechism Devotional: God's Truth for Our Hearts and Minds* (Crossway, 2017)

Tim Keller, *Prayer: Experiencing Awe and Intimacy with God* (Hodder & Stoughton, 2014)

C. S. Lewis, *The Weight of Glory* (William Collins, 2013)

C. S. Lewis, *Mere Christianity* (Collins, 2016)

C. S. Lewis, *Reflections on the Psalms* (HarperOne, 2017)

J. I. Packer, *Knowing God* (Hodder & Stoughton, 2005)

John Piper, *A Hunger for God: Desiring God through Fasting and Prayer* (IVP, 1997)

St Augustine, *The Confessions* (OUP, 2008)

About Keswick Ministries

Our purpose

Keswick Ministries is committed to the spiritual renewal of God's people for his mission in the world.

God's purpose is to bring his blessing to all the nations of the world. That promise of blessing, which touches every aspect of human life, is ultimately fulfilled through the life, death, resurrection, ascension and future return of Christ. All of the people of God are called to participate in his missionary purposes, wherever he may place them. The central vision of Keswick Ministries is to see the people of God equipped, encouraged and refreshed to fulfil that calling, directed and guided by God's Word in the power of his Spirit, for the glory of his Son.

Our priorities

Keswick Ministries seeks to serve the local church through:

- **Hearing God's Word**: the Scriptures are the foundation for the church's life, growth and mission, and Keswick Ministries is committed to preaching and teaching God's Word in a way that is faithful to Scripture and relevant to Christians of all ages and backgrounds.

- **Becoming like God's Son**: from its earliest days the Keswick movement has encouraged Christians to live godly lives in the power of the Spirit, to grow in Christlikeness and to live under his lordship in every area of life. This is God's will for his people in every culture and generation.

- **Serving God's mission**: the authentic response to God's Word is obedience to his mission, and the inevitable result of Christlikeness is sacrificial service. Keswick Ministries seeks to encourage committed discipleship in family life, work and society, and energetic engagement in the cause of world mission.

Our ministry

- **Keswick: the event**. Every summer the town of Keswick hosts a three-week convention, which attracts some 15,000 Christians from the UK and around the world. The event provides Bible teaching for all ages, vibrant worship, a sense of unity across generations and denominations, and an inspirational call to serve Christ in the world. It caters for children of all ages and has a strong youth and young adult programme. And it all takes place in the beautiful Lake District – a perfect setting for rest, recreation and refreshment.

- **Keswick: the movement**. For 140 years the work of Keswick has had an impact on churches worldwide, and today the movement is underway throughout the UK, as well as in many parts of Europe, Asia, North America, Australia, Africa and the Caribbean. Keswick Ministries is committed to strengthening the network in the UK and beyond, through prayer, news, pioneering and cooperative activity.

- **Keswick resources**. Keswick Ministries produces a range of books and booklets based on the core foundations of Christian life and mission. It makes Bible teaching available through free access to MP3 downloads, and the sale of DVDs and CDs. It broadcasts online through Clayton TV and annual BBC Radio 4 services.

- **Keswick teaching and training**. In addition to the summer convention, Keswick Ministries is developing teaching and training events that will happen at other times of the year and in other places.

Our unity

The Keswick movement worldwide has adopted a key Pauline statement to describe its gospel inclusivity: 'for you are all one in Christ Jesus' (Galatians 3:28). Keswick Ministries works with evangelicals from a wide variety of church backgrounds, on the understanding that they share a commitment to the essential truths of the Christian faith as set out in its statement of belief.

Our contact details

T: 01768 780075
E: info@keswickministries.org
W: www.keswickministries.org
Mail: Keswick Ministries, Rawnsley Centre, Main Street, Keswick, Cumbria CA12 5NP, England

Related titles from IVP

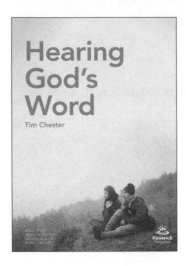

KESWICK STUDY GUIDE

Hearing God's Word
Tim Chester

ISBN: 978–1–78359–581–5
80 pages, paperback

What has God said? How has he said it? And how does it apply to our lives today?

Hearing God's Word invites us to explore these questions and more.

Each session starts with an introduction to the topic and then moves to a Bible passage. We focus on the theme, go deeper and explore living out the word in our daily life. Useful prayer prompts also help to make the message real and personal.

Praise:

'Biblical, practical, devotional and thoughtful. An excellent resource for group or personal study to strengthen our convictions about the truth of the Bible, and enable us to discover its riches for ourselves.' **John Risbridger**

'Here is a workable, practical guide that will help you to study the Bible by yourself or with others. Used well, it will help you grow in your faith.' **Ian Coffey**

Available from your local Christian bookshop or **www.ivpbooks.com**

Related titles from IVP

KESWICK FOUNDATIONS

Sent
Serving God's Mission

Tim Chester

ISBN: 978 1 78359 654 6
80 pages, paperback

Mission is for everyone. Ordinary people can step out to become part of the most exciting, amazing, continuing adventure in the history of the world. Mission begins on our doorstep, but it reaches far beyond. It involves praying, giving and going.

Sent: Serving God's Mission offers a job description. We go right back to the character of God and see how the concept of mission unfolds throughout the storyline of the Bible.

Praise:

'Tim is one of the world's clearest and most compelling mission teachers . . . [here is] a treasure trove for us to take back to our families and home groups.' **Anna Bishop**

'I love the way this study guide so clearly teaches us the Bible, to encourage us to reach out to the world in evangelism.' **Rico Tice**

Available from your local Christian bookshop or **www.ivpbooks.com**